with

Coping

GROWTH SPURTS AND DELAYED GROWTH

James W. Fiscus

The Rosen Publishing Group, Inc.
New York

Published in 2002 by The Rosen Publishing Group, Inc.
29 East 21st Street, New York, NY 10010

Cover © Zefa Visual Media/Index Stock Imagery

Library of Congress Cataloging-in-Publication Data

Fiscus, James.
Coping with growth spurts and delayed growth / James W. Fiscus.—1st ed.
p. cm. — (Coping)   7 / 1 5 0 7 7
Includes bibliographical references and index.
Summary: Explores the physical growth that occurs in adolescence, physical and emotional difficulties that can accompany growth spurts, and the rare but serious growth-related medical conditions that can occur.
ISBN 0-8239-3508-6 (library binding)
1. Human growth—Juvenile literature. 2. Puberty—Juvenile literature.
3. Growth disorders—Juvenile literature. [1. Growth. 2. Puberty.
3. Growth disorders.] I. Title. II. Series.
QP84 .F487 2001
612.6'61—dc21

                                                                2001004721

Manufactured in the United States of America

Contents

Introduction

Most of us want to be the same as our friends. We want to fit in. Even as we learn to be individuals and to think for ourselves rather than to follow a group, we are afraid of being different. We are afraid that if we are different, we will be alone. But in the end, we are all different in one way or another.

In any class at school, some of your friends will be taller than most kids and some will be shorter. Kids grow at different speeds and can start their major growth spurts years apart. Students in middle school or high school who are growing normally can be many inches—even a foot or more—different in height. Generally, girls reach their adult height several years before boys do.

Our major growth spurt begins shortly after the start of puberty. When we look at the normal growth range for girls and boys, there can be a difference of six years between a girl who started puberty on the young end of the normal range and a boy who started at the older end of the range. As a result, one person can be nearly an adult physically while the other is just beginning to grow out of childhood (of course, there can also be girls who start late and boys who start early). Put all this together, and on average girls reach their adult height by age fifteen while boys do not do so until age eighteen.

There is only one absolute rule about growth: We are all different.

Each of us has the tendency to distrust people who appear to be different from ourselves. If we understand why we are different, we can move beyond distrust and fear and accept other individuals—and ourselves—for who they are and who we are. If we understand how we grow and develop, that understanding can help us cope with the changes of growing.

This book looks at how and why human beings grow as they do, and examines the biological process of growth. Also discussed are the differences between male and female growth, and what you can expect to experience during your growth spurt.

We all grow in basically the same way. At the same time, we all grow differently. We are individuals. The term "normal" is used throughout this book in the context of growth and development. In this context, normal refers to the most common range of growth and development and to the absence of a specific medical issue. People can be shorter or taller than most of their peers because of their genetics and be completely within a medically "normal" growth range.

However, extremely short stature or tall stature can indicate a medical problem leading to a form of either dwarfism or gigantism. Today, both can generally be treated, if not prevented, and many of the physical problems that accompany these conditions can be helped. In the case of some conditions, such as Marfan's syndrome, treatment is vital to prevent early death.

This book also discusses some of the other changes that come with puberty and some of the things you will need to consider, such as hygiene, diet, and exercise. The focus, however, will also be on physical growth.

Above all, this book tries to help you understand how you are growing and the changes that happen as you grow. The period of rapid growth that comes with puberty is nearly always an awkward time. The hormones that drive growth and sexual development also throw our emotions off kilter. It takes time to understand what is happening to us. Physically, we do not feel the same. We are different than we have been throughout our lives. Becoming comfortable with our adult bodies, minds, and hormones takes time and understanding. This book cannot give you time, but it may help you understand.

How We Grow

Zoe and Lillie are twins, but not identical twins. While both of their parents are a bit shorter than average, Zoe is about average height. Lillie is somewhat shorter and slighter than average. Both girls are near the top of their classes academically.

When they were in middle school, Zoe remembers that as they walked home, a boy from their school came up to Lillie and hit her on the head, calling her short and dumb. The twins' older brother, Sean, rushed to their defense and the bully fled.

"Being called short and dumb is really hard," Lillie said, remembering the hurt it caused her. Lillie has not forgotten the teasing years ago, but she has not let it affect her life. She knows who she is and what she wants to do.

"Everybody is taller than somebody else, and everybody is shorter than somebody, and that's true all our lives. But not everybody gets a chance to make friends with other people," Zoe said. "One reason we sometimes don't get a chance to make friends with someone is that while they are a really nice person, they look at us and say we are too tall or too short."

"That really hurts the person who's being a snob and a bully more than it does the kid they snub," Lillie

said. "They're the ones who lose by not making a friend."

"Some people are cool with how tall they are and they love it," Zoe said. "That's good. Lillie is shorter than the other kids in her class, but she doesn't care." Zoe paused, thinking. "No, there's one creep who calls her Shrimp. We'd both like to punch him out when he does that."

"He's the only one who does it anymore," Lillie said, scowling a moment before lightening the tone of her voice. "If you're smaller than someone else, it means you can go into places that taller people can't. You can do more sometimes. Being small is a good thing. But I still want to know why we grow. I wonder why we can't be as small as we were when we were babies. It might be a lot more fun."

The Basics of How We Grow

Human beings evolved over millions of years, as did all other forms of life. Plants, animals, and other life forms evolve through natural selection. Natural selection and evolution sound like complex ideas, but they are really fairly elegant ideas. (Scientists say an idea is "elegant" when it clearly explains a complex process.)

Children and teens want to know about themselves. They often ask, Why do we grow at all? The fast answer is that we grow because it would be impossible for a mother to give birth to an adult-sized child who would be as big as she was. The wider question Lillie asked is, Why do we grow as we do? One part of the answer comes from understanding genetics and cell growth. The other part to the answer comes from understanding evolution and natural selection. The way in which plants and animals evolve, and what our eyes see, helps us understand why we grow tall.

Genetics and Cell Growth

Everything about our physical makeup—the color of our eyes, hair, and skin, and how tall we are—comes from information stored in our genes. Genes are part of the cells that make up our bodies. At the center of each cell is a nucleus, and in that nucleus are our genes. Genes are made of DNA, the chemicals from which all life is built. Genes are organized in the nucleus on twenty-three threadlike pairs of structures called chromosomes. The information carried in parents' genes is their children's genetic inheritance, the basic information about what kind of individuals the children will be. Our genetic makeup also largely determines how fast we will grow and when our growth spurt will begin.

Evolution and Natural Selection

Two animals that live on the plains of Africa—the zebra and the giraffe—are perfect examples of evolution and natural selection at work. Despite both animals living on the African plains, a place of grasslands with scattered trees, giraffes and zebras are very different animals. Their physical makeup shows each animal's ability to adapt to the environment in which they live.

Adult zebras are between four and five feet tall at their shoulders (the top joints of their front legs) and look like striped horses, with the males slightly larger than the females.

Adult male giraffes are between nine and eleven feet tall at their shoulders. But their necks are what really tell us that a giraffe is a giraffe. A male giraffe's neck can be nine feet long, and sometimes even longer, bringing their full height to eighteen feet. Female giraffes are about two feet shorter. Giraffes are nearly four times taller than zebras, yet they live in the same type of country. Why? The answer lies in what they eat.

Giraffes eat the leaves of bushes and trees. Zebras graze on ground grasses. Giraffes that were taller and had longer necks had an advantage over shorter giraffes when it came to eating leaves from tall trees. Zebras, on the other hand, benefited from remaining short so that they could easily eat grass. Giraffes that were tall enough to reach up for their food and zebras that were the right height to reach down for their food were more likely to pass their genes on to their young. Over millions of years, the bodies of these animals grew to the point that was best suited to the harsh African environment.

Human Evolution and Growth Spurts

The evolutionary process that works with giraffes and zebras also works with human beings. To be able to pass their genes on to children, however, people must live until they are old enough to bear children. When compared to other people, different traits—how tall they are, how far they can see—made it more likely that an individual would live long enough to reproduce.

Our ancestors were those people who lived long enough to have children. The body, then, had to prepare for its child-bearing abilities, and that meant a genetic triggering of the growing spurt. Then, if an individual had a trait or ability that made him or her more likely to survive, that individual was more likely to pass his or her genes on to children. In other words, if being taller rather than shorter helped survival, human beings would tend to become taller from generation to generation.

Sight and Height

One reason we grow as tall as we do has everything to do with our ability to see well. The human eye is very good at detecting motion against a background of vertical lines. In other words, we appear to have evolved to see danger, and food, moving against a background of tall grass. Our eyes are also good at seeing things at a great distance. Some animals use smell or hearing to find things. We mainly use our eyes.

Wild grasses can easily grow four or five feet tall, and being tall enough to see over the top of the grass made it easier to see animals hunting us for food and for us to see animals we, in turn, needed to hunt for food. (This is only part of a complex process, but it is one reason why we are what we are.) Because of where early humans lived, the individuals who were tall enough to see over tall grass were more likely to survive until they had children.

Dynamics of Growth Spurts

While natural selection helps explain why we grow, it does not tell us how we grow. To understand that we have to look at basic biology. For us to grow, our size has to increase. A baby that weighs 7 pounds when it is born can easily weigh 150 or more pounds as an adult, changing from being two feet tall to standing six feet tall.

We have two major growth spurts. During the first year of life, babies usually triple their weight and add about 50 percent to their height. Recent research confirms that babies can grow up to an inch in a single day, so there are growth spurts within growth spurts. The second growth spurt comes with puberty when we gain about 20 percent of our adult height. Between the two spurts, growth is fairly steady, though even during this period children can experience very rapid bursts of growth. How can that happen?

Cell Division and Growth

For us to grow and have more muscle, more bone, more skin, and larger organs, the number of cells that make up our bodies must increase. (Nerve cells are different, but they do not add much to our overall size.) Cells reproduce themselves through mitosis, the splitting of a single cell into two new cells. The new cells then grow to the size of their parent. After they grow, they each split into two more cells. Two cells become four. The four cells rest and grow, and split again. Four cells become eight. Eight become sixteen, and so on.

During mitosis, the nucleus of the parent cell—and the chromosomes and genes within the nucleus—divide first, so that each new cell contains half of the original nucleus. Bones, muscle, skin, teeth, and all the other tissue in our bodies (except for nerve cells) grow because the cells that build the tissue reproduce by means of mitosis.

Bone Growth

Bones grow in several ways. They increase in thickness as we grow because calcium is added to the bones. At the same time, calcium increases bone density, making them strong and hard. (Increasing density means that an object of the same size contains more matter. For example, a cubic foot of popcorn is much less dense than a cubic foot of iron.) Bones grow longer when a thin growth plate near the end of the bones creates more bone. The growth plates are called epiphyseal plates, or the epiphysis. In the case of the broad, rounded bones of our skulls and some other bones, the growth plates increase their diameter as they form around the edges of the bones.

Bones are hard tissue, and if they pressed directly against each other they would act like two rocks rubbing together and quickly wear down. To protect and cushion our bones, there are soft pads of cartilage at their ends. In addition to cushioning, cartilage gives the shape to other parts of our body. The hard tissue that gives our ears their funnel shape is also cartilage.

Bones and Body Height

The amount of growth is different for different types of bone. You might think that tall people get most of their height from the length of their spines. That is incorrect. The thirty-three vertebrae that form the human spine only double in growth from infancy to adulthood. In a baby, each vertebra is about an inch long, while in an adult each is only a couple of inches long.

The majority of our adult height is determined by the growth and overall length of our leg bones. The long bones of our legs and arms can easily grow four times as large between infancy and adulthood. Much of this growth comes during the two major growth spurts. That's why you may have changed from a pant length of twenty-five to twenty-eight or even thirty over a single summer.

In long bones, the growth plate is between the outer pad of cartilage and the shaft of bone. The shaft is also called the diaphysis. The diaphysis is a thick cylinder of hard, compact bone around a central cavity that holds the bone marrow. The growth plates on each end of the long bones change cartilage into bone, adding bone to the shaft. The growth plate produces cartilage on its outer edge and converts it into bone that is added on its inner surface. As a result, the bone grows longer and we grow taller.

The growth plates are active and add new bone during childhood and adolescence. As most of us become adults, our growth stops because the growth plates harden and become bone themselves (the exception is gigantism, discussed in chapter 6).

Hormones and Growth Control

Hormones are chemicals produced by glands in one part of the body that enter the blood stream to cause changes in another part of the body. Hormones direct and control much of what happens to us, including normal growth and growth spurts.

Several hormones control when we grow and how tall we grow. The most important of these is human growth hormone (GH or hGH), which is produced by the pituitary gland. The pituitary gland is a pea-sized gland located in a cavity at the base of the skull. It is the master endocrine gland, directing the action of many other glands in the body. The pituitary itself takes its orders from a part of the brain called the hypothalamus.

The growth hormone from the pituitary stimulates production of a related hormone in the liver, which in turn stimulates bone growth. Growth is also influenced by the thyroid hormone, which is produced by the thyroid gland in the throat. These and other hormones work both individually and in combination to control how we grow. The growth process illustrates one of the mechanisms through which hormones act. Rather than acting directly (in our example, on the growth plate), a hormone produced by one gland may stimulate another gland to produce a second hormone that then causes a change in the body. The chain of actions by which the hypothalamus stimulates the pituitary to produce GH, which in turn stimulates the liver to produce its growth-related hormone that then stimulates bone growth, is called a cascading action. The term "cascading action" is applied to many situations outside of the body as well.

GH is produced by the pituitary throughout our lives, but the body's reaction to it changes when we become adults. Instead of controlling how tall we become, it guides our bodies in using proteins. Too much growth hormone (hypersecretion) can lead to gigantism, while too little (hyposecretion) can lead to short stature or dwarfism. A number of problems can cause either condition. During puberty, the growth plates slowly harden in response to the sex hormones being produced in increasing amounts. If the plates did not harden, we would all continue to grow, as do people with gigantism.

All the Parts Work Together

When we look at the full picture, our growth results from a complex set of environmental and evolutionary factors that led to the development of modern human beings. Physiologically, we grow because of a number of other complex factors. How tall we are is guided by how tall our parents are, as our genes provide the overall guideline for our appearance, and by factors such as nutrition and our overall health. In the end, it is the complex interaction of all these elements that makes us the individuals we are.

The Differences We Face

"I've always been tall," said Shawna. Shawna is well over six feet tall. She has gotten used to walking with a hunch to avoid hitting the tops of doors.

"I knew I was going to be really tall when I was in kindergarten. I went out to the playground and climbed on the bars of the jungle gym. The other kids were swinging upside down by their knees. When I tried to hang by my knees, my head hit the ground."

"I wasn't that tall that early," Zack said. "I'm seventeen now, and about six-and-a-half-feet tall. I grew pretty steadily, without real spurts. I haven't been teased much. Sure, everybody asks if I play basketball, and expects me to. I don't take it seriously, and tell them that I play soccer and tennis instead."

"I started puberty early and grew even taller," Shawna said. "Most of the other girls, and about all the boys, were short compared to me. I was teased a lot. Sometimes, it was pretty bad. I don't think most of the kids realized how much their teasing hurt me, but some of them wanted to be vicious. They wanted to hurt other people."

"I was lucky," Zack said. "I was not as tall as Shawna, and that may be why the teasing wasn't that bad for me. I never took it seriously. I don't know why, but it didn't get to me. Besides, being tall is easier for a boy. My friends all tend to be tall, though. It's just easier hanging with them. I'd say they were all in the top 5 percent in height."

Shawna sat in her chair, hunched a bit. "The teasing got to me. I know that I'm a lot shyer than I would have been if I'd been more average height and not as tall. A lot of that depends on the people you go to school with. A lot of it is how you deal with it. I didn't do as well as Zack. But I'm changing. I'm forcing myself not to be as shy." She paused. "No, I'll always be shy, but I don't have to let it keep me from having friends. I don't have to let the fact that I'm tall keep me off by myself all the time."

"You shouldn't let things get to you," Zack told Shawna. "I have a friend who is very short. Especially when he stands by me." Zack smiled. "He gets in fights. A lot. It's not just that he's short, he also has a heavy East Coast accent and a lisp that stands out here in Seattle. He's very aggressive, and won't take stuff from anyone.

"He needs to find something that he's good at so that he knows he's not a loser," Zack went on. "Being tall or being short doesn't change who we are or what we can do. Stay active. I play the guitar, and that helps me meet people. I'm also in a band. Nothing big, but it's a lot of fun."

The Growth Spurt at Puberty

Our growth spurt during puberty accounts for about 20 percent of our adult height, and it is usually spread over a relatively short period of time. That kind of quick growth can truly toss you off balance. Before you hit puberty, you already have become used to walking and running with the body size that you have. The length of your legs and torso are of a size with which you are comfortable. You are also used to how much you weigh, and how to balance your weight when you walk or run. Now, all of that is changing quickly.

Within one summer's time, you can grow three inches or more. Your feet can grow three sizes larger than before. This growth spurt puts your new size at odds with what your brain remembers of your shorter body. During this time you find yourself tripping over your own feet, or taking long, slow strides with your longer legs. Don't worry. This is perfectly normal. It will take time for your instincts to catch up to your changing body.

Which Body Parts Grow Fastest?

While girls usually start their growth spurt at a younger age than boys and achieve their adult height at a younger age, the overall process of growth is the same for both boys and girls. The first areas that show dramatic growth are the hands and feet. As a result, your hands and feet will grow larger before your arms, legs, and torso catch up. You will outgrow your shoes before you outgrow your jackets and jeans. Often you will feel awkward both in looks and movement.

Height and Weight

Before puberty, the average boy or girl grows about two or two and a half inches a year. During puberty, growth can be dramatically faster, sometimes three or four inches a year. At times, a spurt within the main growth spurt can increase height by an inch within a few weeks. During our puberty growth spurt, we grow nine or ten inches on average, with a general range between four to twelve inches. That growth happens within a two or three year period.

We also have a period of rapid weight gain as we grow taller. That's mostly because our bones are becoming larger and denser, but we are also adding muscle and other tissues as we grow. It is not at all unusual to put on twenty pounds in a year early in the growth spurt. Both boys and girls also tend to put on weight before one of the minispurts, then shoot up in height. The cycle of moderate weight gain followed by growth is normal and essential for proper growth. While you do not want to let yourself become too overweight, it is very important to understand that gaining weight is part of growing.

Girls and Growth

"My breasts started to develop when I was about nine," Janna said, *"and I had my first period when I was eleven. I was the first girl in my class to start growing.*

"I didn't know what was happening at first, because my mom passed away and my dad didn't talk to me about that stuff at all. A lot of my friends changed in how they treated me. I heard them giggling behind my back. Some of the girls called me a whore just 'cause I had boobs when they didn't.

"I wasn't having sex or anything," Janna said, *falling silent for a moment. "I'm sixteen and I'm still a virgin, so I'm doing pretty good. I didn't let their comments control me.*

"I had a lot of trouble when my period started, but only because I didn't know what to do. One of my teachers realized what was going on and helped. She filled me in on what I had to do and what was happening. That made it a lot easier.

"But I still walked hunched over and wore baggy tops to hide my breasts. I only stopped doing that when other girls in my class started to develop, too," Janna said. *"It feels strange now that the others girl are*

*catching up with me. Some of the ones who called me
a slut have even asked me what kind of tampons I use.
I'm not friends with the ones who were the worst, but
most of them are OK."*

Janna's troubles are common for girls who develop more
quickly than their peers. There is a wide belief that girls
start puberty when they have their first menstrual period—
called menarche—but this is not true. Medically, puberty
in girls is defined as the onset of breast development,
which is the first sign that they are producing the female
sex hormone estrogen.

It takes time for the uterus, after it is exposed to estrogen
with the start of puberty, to develop to the point that a girl
can start cycling with her menstrual period. Menarche happens from one year to three years after the start of puberty.

Is Puberty Starting at a Younger Age?

Girls in the United States and Canada (and possibly boys as
well) seem to be starting puberty at a younger age than their
grandmothers (and grandfathers) did. For most of the twen-
tieth century, the average age for the start of puberty in girls
appears to have been about a year older than it is now. The
question, however, is still being debated by doctors as new
studies are done and historical records are reviewed. Some
historical sources appear to confuse the start of puberty with
a girl's first menstrual period, which comes later, and their
confusion has helped cloud the issue.

For girls in the United States, the average age for the start
of puberty today is around ten. African American girls tend
to start puberty slightly earlier than Caucasian girls, for rea-

sons that are not yet understood. Doctors say that the normal range for the start of puberty is two to two and a half years either way from the average. The range, then, for the normal start of puberty is about eight to thirteen. With a normal range of five years for the start of puberty, there is a great difference in where girls (or boys, as we will see) of the same age might be in their growth cycle and how tall they might be.

Turning back to the earlier onset of puberty, some researchers suggest that the increased presence of compounds in our environment and foods that mimic the female hormone estrogen may be triggering puberty earlier in girls. The compounds, which come as part of many chemicals used in agriculture and industry, may also be affecting boys and reducing the sperm count among men.

The fact that children are getting better nutrition now than during earlier generations may allow puberty to start at a younger age for both girls and boys (based on the fact that being underweight can delay the start of puberty). If we look back 100 years or so, the average age of puberty for girls was between fifteen and seventeen. It seems likely that poor nutrition was the main reason for their late puberty.

One reason we have trouble being sure puberty is starting at a younger age is because our historical information is not good. If we go back to the Middle Ages (900–1400) in Europe, we know that the religious authority at the time, the Roman Catholic Church, set the marriage age for girls at twelve and for boys at fourteen. If the marriage age was set to match the average age for the start of puberty, that implies that girls then started puberty at about twelve. However, it is likely that rather than dating the start of puberty itself, the marriage age dated the first menstrual period. That could mean that the start of puberty in the Middle Ages was not that different than it is today.

It is hard to miss a girl's first menstrual period, but the first signs of puberty are more subtle. Therefore, even in the modern age we have better information on the average age for the start of menstrual periods than of puberty. For the past fifty years, the average starting age for menstruation has held steady at between twelve and thirteen years of age in the United States. As this book is written, there is good evidence that puberty is starting at a younger age for American and Canadian girls. However, we do not yet know why, or exactly how much earlier. When we look at any body of scientific knowledge, we are always in a position of knowing some things and being uncertain about others.

Nutrition and Puberty
The quality of our diets also can change the age at which we start puberty. Just as better nutrition has led to an increase in our average height, it has helped move the age at which we start puberty younger and younger. Now the average is about ten years old. Also, the amount of body fat we have—which is a result of our diets—can change the start of puberty. A girl must weigh about 100 pounds before she has her first menstrual period, and girls who have faced starvation will experience delayed puberty. Proof of this comes from information gained during and after World War II, based on observations of civilian famine and Holocaust victims.

Puberty and Girls

The first two signs girls usually notice as they begin puberty are the development of their breasts and the growth of pubic hair. Girls also gain weight, increasing body weight by 10 to 20 percent. With both boys and girls, the majority of the weight gain is due to new bone and muscle tissue growth. Girls do increase the proportion of fat in their bodies during puberty, and it is vital that they do so. The main reason for this change is the preparation of a girl's body for pregnancy and childbirth. Fat stores energy, and a woman needs that reservoir of energy if she becomes pregnant.

A girl's weight gain during puberty does *not* mean that she needs to lose weight. If you do not put on the additional weight, which may happen because of dieting or too much exercise, you risk delaying the onset of puberty and menstruation. With the start of puberty, girls' hips also broaden to prepare them for childbirth, making the waist seem smaller in comparison. As with boys, a girl's larynx (voice box) grows and the voice changes. The change in the larynx and vocal cords, however, is not as dramatic as it is with boys, and girls do not develop an "Adam's apple."

Girls tend to have their peak growth spurt early in puberty while boys have their peak growth spurt during the middle to late stages of puberty. Girls, as a result, tend to reach their adult height around fifteen years of age while boys tend to grow for three more years, not reaching their adult height until eighteen. The same five-year range for the start of puberty applies for both boys and girls in reaching their full growth.

Breasts

A girl's breasts usually develop over four or five years, starting when she is between nine and fourteen. When puberty begins, the breasts and nipples rise slightly, forming breast buds. The circles of skin around the nipples, the areolas, become wider and darken. Slowly, the breasts become larger, and the areolas and nipples become small, separate mounds that rise above the breast. Finally, breasts grow round and full. The nipples stick out while the areolas no longer rise above the breast.

Remember, however, that this is the general pattern. The final size and shape of breasts vary widely, depending on many factors. Genetics is the most important factor, but as breasts are in part made up of fatty tissue, the level of a girl's physical activity can affect the size of her breasts. Runners, for example, tend to have small breasts because they have a lower percentage of body fat. Breasts also change in size throughout a girl's menstrual cycle.

It is also common for a girl's breasts to develop at different rates, with the right or left breast larger than the other. Eventually, they usually end up at about the same size. However, it is normal for a woman's breasts to be of slightly different size and shape, as the right and left sides of our bodies are rarely identical. Most people simply are not symmetrical.

There are also wide differences in how breasts look. Areolas vary in color. Nipples vary in shape and the degree to which they stick out, and the overall shape and size of the breasts vary from small to large. Some girls and women have nipples that do not stick out. They are called inverted nipples, and they are not a medical problem. However, if nipples that were not inverted suddenly become so, see your doctor to be sure that there is no medical issue.

Pubic Hair

Before puberty, we do not have pubic hair, with the possible exception of a few fuzzy hairs. When puberty begins, the first real pubic hairs grow. At the start, they are straight and fine. Over time, pubic hairs darken and become coarser. They also become curlier.

By the end of puberty, pubic hair tends to be thick, coarse, and tightly curled. A girl's hair color will affect how thick her pubic hair is. Her racial and ethnic background also influences how much pubic hair she has. Pubic hair is not always the same color as the hair on our heads. For girls and women, pubic hair provides protection for the delicate lips of the vulva.

Some women and girls remove pubic hair that might show when they are wearing a bathing suit. If you decide to do so, be very careful, as shaving can irritate the tender skin of the pubic area. Depilatories (chemicals that remove hair) can also irritate the skin and should be used with care.

Growth Spurts and Sexual Activity

Girls who start puberty at a younger age and develop their breasts and adult shapes earlier than other girls are often accused of being sexually active. There is no connection, however, between early development and the start of sexual activity. It is important for you to remember that how soon you develop and how you react to the changes that are happening to you are two different things. If you develop early, you do not have to start having sex before you are ready to do so. If a friend develops before you do, do not assume—or suggest—that she is having sex.

On the other hand, if you are experiencing delayed growth, stay involved with your friends who are now going through their growth spurts. There is no reason for you to think that you or your friends are suddenly different people. They probably want to talk about their changes as much as you want to discover what and how those changes are affecting them. Whatever the case may be, eventually you will all reach the same point. You will all have passed from childhood into adulthood. No matter how early or late you and other girls are going through puberty, you can still remain friends and help each other by talking about the fears and anxieties that come as part of growing.

Boys and Puberty

Boys, on average, start puberty a year later than do girls. The mean age for the onset of puberty in boys is around eleven or eleven and a half years old. As with girls, boys have a two- to two-and-a-half-year range for the normal start of puberty. Thus, boys start puberty from about age nine up to fourteen. On average, they achieve their adult height at about eighteen years old.

In boys, the first sign of the onset of puberty is subtle. Male puberty begins with the enlarging of the testes, which comes about six months before the growth of pubic hair. The testes are the male sex organs that produce sperm. The testes and the various ducts that support them combine to form the testicles, which in turn are carried in the scrotum (most of the time, we can use the terms "testes" and "testicles" interchangeably). Other structures in the testicles produce the primary male sex hormone, testosterone. Most boys do not notice the first change in the size of their testicles, and puberty in boys is usually thought to start with the first showing of pubic hair.

Penis, Scrotum, and Pubic Hair

The body changes boys notice most during puberty are the development of their genitals. During childhood, a boy's penis, testicles, and scrotum remain fairly small. There is some growth, but it is not dramatic. With the start of puberty, the testes increase in size and the scrotum hangs lower. The testes continue to grow until young men are about age twenty.

The testicles have to remain at a fairly constant temperature for the highest sperm production. If they become either too hot or too cold, the number and quality of the sperm lowers. That is one reason that in warm weather the scrotum hangs lower: to allow for greater cooling, while in cold weather, it tightens toward the body for greater warmth. During the early stages of puberty, the penis may enlarge slightly and pubic hair slowly begins to grow.

During the next stage of puberty, the penis grows noticeably longer while the testicles and scrotum continue to enlarge and develop. As time passes, the penis becomes noticeably thicker. The head of the penis, the glans, becomes more distinct and boys finally have their full growth of pubic hair. Remember that pubic hair may be a different color than the hair on your head. The final adult growth of the male genitals comes at about fifteen, with a general range from thirteen to eighteen.

Facial Hair

Boys also begin to see their beards and mustaches grow during puberty. The amount of facial hair boys have changes gradually during adolescence and young adulthood. The age of beard growth also varies, from the early teen years

25

through the late twenties. Some men never develop a heavy beard. Major hormone imbalance can reduce beard growth and can be treated, but for most of us our genes determine at what age, and how heavily, male beards grow.

Contrary to an old myth, shaving has no permanent impact on hair growth and will not make a beard darker or heavier. Hair does grow more quickly immediately after shaving, but its growth decreases within a few hours. Because hair is darker and coarser at its root, shaving exposes the darker, coarser part of the hair shaft, making the beard look heavier.

The Male Physique

As boys grow, their shoulders and rib cages become broader and they begin to add muscle to their bodies. Their arms become longer, matching their shoulders. The amount of muscle tissue boys have will double during puberty. With the muscle growth, boys become stronger. Most boys grow in height, weight, and amount of muscle at about the same time. Level of strength, however, lags behind growth by about a year. The heart and lungs must also grow stronger and increase their efficiency before boys can build their overall endurance and strength.

Cracking Voice

The larynx also enlarges, providing the Adam's apple that develops in boys but not in girls. During puberty, the vocal cords in the larynx become thicker and longer, resulting in the change in the voice as tones deepen. Sometimes, early in the growth of your larynx, your voice may crack, suddenly shifting to a higher pitch. The cracking of your voice can be very embarrassing, as you want to sound like a man and the high pitch makes you sound like a boy again. Try not to worry about these episodes. Eventually, your vocal cords will grow further and your voice will stop cracking.

Your Changing Body Shape

All of us change our general shapes as we grow. The proportion of our bodies—the amount of our total height that comes from our legs, trunk, and head—changes dramatically. Otherwise, adults would look like huge babies. Remember that the vertebrae of our backbones do little more than double in height as we grow, while the long bones of our legs and arms can easily grow by a factor of four by the time we become adults.

If our backbones and legs grew in the same way, we would have short legs and long trunks compared to our actual appearance. In addition, our heads are much closer to their adult size when we are born then are the rest of our bodies. In terms of the numbers, a baby's head is about one-quarter of total height (or length, as babies cannot stand) and its legs only about three-eighths of total height. With adults, the head accounts for about one-eighth of height while legs give them about half their total height.

For both boys and girls, our faces change as we grow, becoming longer and wider. Our mouths widen, our faces become longer, and our chins jut out more. Our noses also grow longer and wider, and may reach their adult size before the rest of our face does. That means that your nose may seem too big for your face during puberty. All of this change gives teens that gawky appearance everyone talks about, and which they see in themselves and others at school. This is normal, and your features will catch up with the rest of your face.

Impact of the Differences Between Us

We look at ourselves and at our peers, and compare how we are doing. If we do not match what we see, it is easy to label ourselves as abnormal. It is far too easy to decide that we are freaks. But with a boy and a girl who are both sixteen years old, it is easily within the normal range of development for the girl to have started puberty at eight and the boy at fourteen. In many ways, she would physically be an adult while he is just starting to develop his adult body. You will have friends who are "late bloomers" and who start puberty several years later than the general range of kids, and others who start early.

Being different—being an individual in how one grows and develops—is really the only thing that is certain about growing. Some people will seem to be too tall, too short, too fat, or too thin, depending on when and how quickly they are growing. All of the variations can be medically normal, and usually are. In the end, growth averages out, but the tempo—the rate and age of growth—can be frustrating and frightening. Talk to your friends, talk to your parents, talk to your teachers, and try to understand what is happening as you grow.

Growth Spurts and Medical Issues

Some kids do have medical problems that create difficulties with how they grow. If you are much shorter than you and your parents think you should be for your age, or if you are late starting puberty, your doctor should give you a physical examination. If you are below the fifth percentile in growth, you should be tested to see if you have a problem with the production of growth hormone or other hormones. Your physician will also look for possible genetic problems that can lead to short stature (see chapter 5). An X-ray can make sure that there is normal development with your skeletal system. However, 95 percent of kids with short stature are either late bloomers or have short parents. Only about 5 percent will need treatment.

Because conditions like Marfan's syndrome and gigantism can and should be treated, adolescents who are growing very tall or noticeably taller than their brothers and sisters or parents should be examined by their doctors.

Changing Needs As We Grow: Hygiene, Nutrition, and Exercise

"There was a kid in class who stank like a dead possum," said Mustapha. "We'd finish gym class and all head into the shower, and he'd kind of duck under the water and then dry off. I had my next class, biology, with him. His name was Bob. We shared a microscope and I had to stand next to him. I hated that, but I didn't want to say anything to him. For one thing, he was a lot bigger than me, since he had started puberty the year before. He was smart and all, but you couldn't stay around him long.

"I think one of the teachers took him aside and talked to him. Not cutting him down. Next day, Bob used soap and took a real shower." Mustapha turned his head, looking as if he was about to check his own armpit, then caught himself and stopped. "Always thought I didn't stink. Last night, I caught a whiff of my dirty laundry at home."

Hygiene

With both boys and girls, sex hormones (androgens) activate the sweat glands. We need sweat to cool our bodies. But the sweat builds, giving bacteria that lives on our skin food it needs to grow. The byproducts of the bacteria cause body odor.

The odor-causing bacteria especially like the sweat produced by the apocrine sweat glands that are concentrated under the arms and in the crotch, explaining why body odor concentrates in those areas. Our first defense against body odor is to shower or take a bath daily. We also have to be sure to shower after exercise, meaning after gym class or sports. In a few cases, extreme body odor is caused by a medical problem that your doctor can help you with.

You can also use either a deodorant or an antiperspirant to fight normal, daily body odors. Deodorants cover odor caused by sweat. Antiperspirants help prevent perspiration. Either will help you deal with the increased sweat and odor that you will experience as you grow into an adult. If you feel burning or another irritation when using either a deodorant or an antiperspirant, stop using it. Try switching to a brand that uses a different formula. Because antiperspirants stop the body from sweating, they are made of stronger chemicals than are deodorants and may be more irritating. In addition, the chemicals in antiperspirants— generally a compound of aluminum, zirconium, and other ingredients—can discolor and damage your clothes.

It is not necessary for either girls or boys to shave their underarm hair or body hair in order to remain clean. Failing to bathe, however, affects the people around you. You need only remember a time when you rode on an elevator or bus with someone who had not washed—and the stench you had to endure—to understand why daily baths or showers are vital.

Even while making sure to bathe daily, you should not become obsessed with washing. During hot weather, especially if you live in a humid climate, you may indeed want to shower at the start of the day and again before bed, but in most weather once a day is enough. In addition to washing yourself, it is important to not wear clothes that are dirty. It is especially important to change underwear daily. Even if you are clean, your clothes can stink.

Acne and Skin Oils

The changes of puberty are often exciting and wonderful, as you learn new things about yourself. Acne is neither exciting nor wonderful, and can be a constant embarrassment and source of humiliation. Some people only have to fight acne for a couple of years, while others battle it into adulthood.

Acne comes with puberty because the oil glands in the skin become more active during this time. These oil glands are concentrated on the face, chest, back, shoulders, and upper arms, making these parts of the body the major sites of acne. Acne can be caused and made worse by a number of factors, some of which you can control and some you cannot control. Genetics are a determining factor in the type and severity of acne you may experience. If your parents had acne, you are more likely to have it. Stress also can bring on an attack of acne. We can do nothing about our genetics, but we can try to reduce the stress in our lives or find ways to deal with it.

In general, acne forms when skin oil flows into hair follicles (hollow hair shafts) that open on the skin as pores. Skin cells stick together with the oil and can block the pores. Bacteria on the skin's surface grow in the blocked follicle, developing a pimple. Pus accumulates, forming a whitehead. If the follicle remains unblocked, it can still attract dirt and form a blackhead. In either case, you get a pimple, which can put you off psychologically. You may see yourself as ugly or grotesque. You may begin to wonder why other people almost never have acne. These are natural reactions, but you don't have to compound them by dwelling on your growth changes.

Other Causes of Acne

You have greater control over other factors that can bring on acne or make it worse. Use of oily makeup or moisturizers can clog your pores and lead to attacks. Also, if you let your hair remain dirty, especially if it comes down over your forehead, you are more likely to have trouble with acne because the dirt and oils in hair can clog your pores.

Acne Prevention and Care

While none of us can completely prevent acne, we can try and reduce the number and severity of attacks. Washing with warm water and a mild soap several times a day can help. Do not scrub too hard, however, as you can damage your skin and cause more trouble than you prevent. A cotton ball or pad dipped in an astringent (an astringent draws the tissues together and stops the flow of the oil) can help control the oils that clog pores. You can do this during the day to remove oil that accumulates on the skin. You can also use a tissue to blot off excess oil. If you use makeup or moisturizers, choose ones that are free of oils and that are labeled as not contributing to acne. Remember to remove any makeup you wear every night.

In addition, while it is important to use a sunblock to protect your skin, try to avoid using an oil-based block. Even if you use a lotion, be sure to wash your face with soap when you come inside from the sun.

If you have severe acne with more than a few pimples, see your doctor. There are prescription medicines and medical treatments that can help. Because acne can cause permanent scars, you should obtain medical help if your acne is heavy. Some allergic reactions may also appear to be simple acne and should be examined by a physician.

One of the things you should not do is pop or probe a pimple, as doing so can aggravate your acne and cause scarring. Instead, use an astringent such as spirit of camphor or an acne medication to dry out the pimple. It may take longer, but you are less likely to end up with a permanent scar.

The zits on your face seem as large as meteor craters on the face of the moon when you look in the mirror. But they are not. Almost everyone gets acne during puberty, and most people continue having minor trouble with it throughout life. That means we are all together as sufferers.

Acne and African American Skin Complexion

African Americans must be careful in treating acne. Abrasive soap and scrubbing devices will not clear up your acne and may damage your skin. They can discolor dark complexions, leading to permanently lighter or darker patches. African American skin is also more likely than the skin of people of lighter complexion to form keloids. A keloid is an abnormal scar tissue that is hard and irregular and that may increase in size. Keloids also form in reaction to injuries, including cuts and burns. Be careful when shaving or treating acne.

Nutrition

People living in industrialized parts of the world today—including North America, Europe, and Japan—are approximately four inches (about ten centimeters) taller than people who lived 150 years ago. Better nutrition is the main reason for this increase in average height. The lesson is that eating right is vital for proper growth. While that is true for our childhood and adolescence, it is most important during our two major growth spurts, including the one you are dealing with now.

A rapidly growing and developing body needs a diet that includes a good mix of the major food types: milk products for calcium; fruits and vegetables for vitamins and minerals; grains for complex carbohydrates, fiber, vitamins, and minerals; and high-quality protein from meat, poultry, fish, eggs, or high-protein legumes. You also need to eat fats—in moderation. The best fats come from unsaturated oils such as olive oil. A balanced diet and moderation are key.

That said, you should also take a multivitamin to supplement your diet. Teens often do not get the best nutrition from eating because their diets are filled with fast-food products and snack munchies. Adding a supplemental multivitamin is an excellent way to ensure your daily vitamin and mineral needs.

Eating and Weight Gain

We are facing two contradictory trends in our world today. Nearly all industrialized nations are in the midst of a fat epidemic. Our economic privileges allow us to purchase whatever foods we wish. Unfortunately, those foods are often filled with fat while offering little nutrition for our bodies' health. Obesity has risen as our economies have become richer. This trend is even worse for teens, who have more spending money at the same time they are bombarded with fast-food commercials. Teenage obesity is becoming a real medical concern, and it begins during the greatest growth spurt that our bodies experience.

Obesity strips you of energy and shortens your life. Obesity kills because it puts a strain on your heart and body that brings early death. Maintaining a normal body weight allows your heart to pump blood through your arteries and veins without being overworked.

Weight and Beauty

Maintaining a weight that is medically normal for our height is not, primarily, a matter of how we look. When we talk of beauty, we speak of appearance only. The variety of people who are thin, normal weight, and overweight can all be beautiful-looking people. Do not, however, confuse appearance with health.

Undereating and Undernourishment

Trying too hard to be thin is just as bad as overeating and obesity. Anorexia nervosa is an eating disorder in which people starve themselves, sometimes to death. The psychological reasons for anorexia are still being debated.

People with anorexia have a distorted image of their bodies. That means that no matter how thin they become, they look in the mirror and think they are fat. Girls are in greater danger of developing anorexia than are boys, and one study found that girls with anorexia estimate their bodies to be 74 percent larger than they actually are. They no longer recognize the reality before them: They are starving themselves and threatening their lives.

Bulimia is related to anorexia, but involves gorging on large meals and then vomiting (purging) to get rid of the food before the body can absorb calories. People with bulimia may also use laxatives, diet pills, or other amphetamine-like drugs to keep off weight by suppressing their appetite. They may also exercise compulsively. (Anorexics may become bulimics, but seldom do bulimics stop eating and become anorexic.)

Bulimics are generally overweight. However, the constant eating and purging unbalances their bodies' electrolyte and chemical balance. This often leads to severe depression. Bulimia can kill, with most of the deaths resulting from heart or kidney failure. Bulimics also choke and suffocate when their own vomit lodges in their throats.

Moderation and balance are best when it comes to eating. Being comfortable with your body, regardless of your weight and appearance, also goes a long way to helping you maintain proper eating habits. After all, you want to have the good health and the energy to be able to enjoy life. Your doctor can help you face and overcome obesity, bulimia, and anorexia.

Exercise

Now is the time for you to develop the habit of exercising to help keep your body in good health. Some people are lucky, and have jobs that keep them active. Most of us are not as lucky, spending more and more time sitting and allowing our bodies to soften and gain fatty tissue.

Exercises are divided into three main types depending on how they affect the body and how the body is used.

All are important for good health, and it is vital to keep them in balance so that we build our muscles, condition our hearts, and develop physical endurance. The best time to begin an exercise habit is during your puberty growth spurt, so your body can grow to its greatest potential and strength during the two years or so it takes to achieve your adult body growth. Your body will react well to exercise during these years. That excess energy you sometimes feel from all those hormonal surges is siphoned off during a good workout. At the same time, you will develop endurance that will help you through those "down" days. Best of all, your body will be toned, and your diet will be put to its best use.

Aerobic Exercise

Aerobic exercise builds our endurance and keeps our hearts and lungs working properly. It requires us to keep our heart rates up through running, swimming, walking quickly, or riding a bike. Any other form of continuous activity will also do the job. There is fairly wide agreement that you should do an aerobic exercise for at least thirty minutes three times a week. That is very little time and effort to put into having a healthy, strong body.

Weight Training

Building strength through exercises that require us to lift weights helps to keep muscles and bones in good condition. Weightlifting is designed to build muscle, plain and simple. Look at it this way: Your body is getting taller, wider, and bigger, so why not make it stronger and look good, and make yourself feel good at the same time? The best benefit of weightlifting is that it gives you a body that performs well under the physical and emotional stress that is part of everyday life.

Stretching Exercises

Stretching exercises keep muscles flexible and bodies and joints loose so that we can move freely and avoid injury. When you stretch, do so gently. If you cause pain, you are likely causing injury. As you stretch, allow your body to move easily and smoothly. Avoid bouncing your stretches (repeatedly pushing into the stretch). Hold each stretch for at least thirty seconds; try to work up to holding it for a minute.

Stretching is very important before and after other exercise. Before, it helps prepare your body for the work it is about to do, while stretching after exercise helps you cool down and avoid stiffness and cramps. Make sure you warm your body up with a fast walk (swing your arms, too) before stretching.

Safe Weight Training

As long as we live, weight-bearing exercises will cause our bones to become denser and stronger. However, lifting weights that are too heavy during puberty may damage the bones, and the ligaments and tendons that connect bones and muscles. You could also damage the growth plates at the end of your long bones, and that would affect your growth.

Keep in mind when looking at someone who is buff that there is a great difference in muscles that are mainly for show and those that are developed for actual use. Compare the body of an Olympic gymnast or acrobat to that of a weightlifter, for example. The weightlifter is massively strong, but the gymnast is both strong and flexible. The gymnast's muscles and body are more versatile.

The latest research indicates that strength training can be done safely, even by kids as young as seven. Any program you start needs to be carefully designed to match your age, build, experience, and the sport for which you are preparing your body. Supervision by someone who knows weight training guidelines and how to match your program to your development and needs is very important.

Do not just sit down at weight equipment and start lifting. Weight training best benefits those who know and use proper lifting techniques. Equally important, failure to use good techniques can lead to injury. Remember also that you can build strength by numerous repetitions using lesser weights, and you are not as likely to injure yourself. It is a good idea to talk to your doctor before starting a serious program.

Guarding Against Overuse Injuries

Overuse injuries are caused by repeated stress on the same muscle or joint during exercise. Throwing a ball or swinging your arm again and again can cause damage, as many baseball and softball pitchers, as well as tennis players, have learned. Shin splints (severe pain along the front edge of your leg) are a similar injury caused by overuse.

The same injuries that were once locker-room talk of sports professionals are now common for exercise enthusiasts, high school athletes, and everyday sports nuts. Stress fractures, tendonitis (inflammation of the tendons), and bursitis (inflammation of the small sacs filled with liquid that help cushion joints) are some other injuries that teens experience today. Avoiding these injuries requires care during sports play. The key is to not overwork your muscles or joints by playing the sport for extended periods of time. Also, practicing at full speed—using the full force of your muscles and joints every time—can cause fatigue and overuse, and may eventually cause damage.

Overall, the thing to remember is that pain is the way your body tells you it has been injured. We all get minor aches and pains from activity. Bruises and strains are part of life. But "playing through the pain" is in almost all cases a bad idea. Ignoring severe pain can lead to an injury that will lay you up for months or even years. Take it easy. The idea of exercise and sports play is to do it in a way that you can keep doing throughout your life.

Growing Pains and Other Issues

"I was late growing; late starting puberty," Leah said. Leah is now a senior in high school. She sat drinking a cola and picking at the fries left over from her lunch as she remembered. "When I was in ninth grade, a friend who was growing faster than I was gave me some of her skirts that she'd outgrown.

"The hems were uneven when I put them on, but they would looked great on her. That was the first time I knew something was wrong. My hips were not even. One was higher than the other. A little later, I was playing touch football at recess, and somebody knocked me down hard. I've always been athletic and didn't think about it. But my back muscles swelled up and were very painful."

Leah told her parents about her injury. "We thought it might be growing pains, but when the swelling didn't go away, we had X rays taken. I was told I have scoliosis— my spine is badly curved. Kind of an S curve. Sure, I'd known my back was a little funny, but I didn't think anything about it.

"The first thing they did was to put me in a body cast for about a week, hoping to straighten out my spine. That was a long week. Nothing happened, though. The cast didn't help. I was too old, and my spine was no longer malleable. The brace couldn't force my spine out of its curve to make it straight again.

"I'm still living with the curved spine and staying active—running, skiing, biking and all," Leah said. "But the scoliosis meant that my hips were uneven and the X-ray showed a cyst, a hollow place, in my hip bone. They had to operate to fix that or my hip could have broken if I'd fallen.

"I was on crutches for six months. They operated early in the summer, and I had a couple of months to practice using my crutches. When tenth grade started, there was a girl who had just broken her leg, and a football player who was also on crutches. We had crutch races in the halls." Leah grinned, remembering. "The football player thought he would beat me easily, but I had two months of practice. I beat everybody, even healthy kids who borrowed somebody's crutches.

"I painted racing stripes on my crutches. Friends at school got racing stickers, the kind you see on the professional racing cars, and we put them on my crutches, and on my pack. Like I said, I still have a curved spine, but I'm as active as I ever was. Sometimes a muscle slips out of place and it really hurts. I don't think, though, that it's bad enough to mean I'll have an operation."

Growing Pains

Growing pains are muscle pains that come and go, often showing up in the late afternoon, evening, or at night. Sometimes, they can wake you during sleep. Some physicians claim that pain experienced during the day is not due to growing pains.

The pain most often strikes the legs, thighs, and behind the knees. It will sometimes appear in the arms, back, groin, shoulders, or ankles, but generally concentrates in the lower limbs. The pain is deep in the muscle tissue and not centered on joints or in an acute location, as it would be with a torn muscle or tendon. Growing pains can affect kids during both childhood and adolescence. They may strike boys more than girls, and in boys are most common at about age thirteen.

Diagnosing Growing Pains

The three most important points about growing pains are that they are real, we do not really know what causes them, and they generally do not indicate a serious medical problem. When we get to the core of the issue, however, growing pains are diagnosed by excluding other conditions that might be more serious.

If you experience persistent muscle pain concentrated in a specific area (lower legs, thighs, behind the knee), see your doctor so a full diagnosis can eliminate or identify a more serious medical problem. For example, a mild case of Osgood-Schlatter disease (discussed below) can be mistaken for simple growing pains.

Sometimes physicians will tell patients that growing pains involve bones and joints stretching a little bit. This explanation gives patients a reason for their discomfort. The latest research, however, points away from a connection between growing pains and growth. Growing pains seem to actually decline during a growth spurt and the site of the pain does not correspond to growth sites.

Injury and Growing Pains

There is also a lot of talk among doctors today claiming growing pains may be caused by a bruise that was not noticed until the boy or girl goes to bed. This seems to explain why growing pains appear mostly toward evening and at night. Doctors claim that when you are awake, your other muscles act as splints and often prevent an injury from being painful. With sleep, you relax and the injury causes pain. Also argued is the fact that when you are active you tend to not notice minor pains.

Growing pains are associated anecdotally (in stories by patients) with periods during growth spurts. When the data is analyzed, however, no direct connection has yet been found to connect rapid growth with growing pains. The unfortunate truth is that we do not yet know what causes growing pains.

The Difference Between Injury and Growing Pains

One way to tell the difference between growing pains and an injury or other condition is to massage or handle the area that hurts. Rubbing or massaging that area tends to relieve the discomfort of growing pains, while it is likely to make an injury or diseased area more painful. Minor injuries will self-heal, but if pain is great you should see a doctor.

Treatment can involve rest of the painful area, massage, application of heat with a heating pad, or taking a pain reliever other than aspirin (aspirin can injure people under the age of fifteen). Acetaminophen (found in Tylenol) and ibuprofen (found in Advil) may help relieve your discomfort. While boys seem to mention trouble with growing pains more than girls do, there is no solid evidence that growing pains are more common with boys.

Osgood-Schlatter Disease

Osgood-Schlatter disease is fairly common in active, growing teens. It is most often seen in boys about twelve or thirteen years old. The disease causes pain and swelling in the knee and affects the upper part of the shin. The inflammation strikes where the tendon from the patella (the kneecap) attaches to the upper tibia (shin bone). The bone is still fairly soft during growth, and it is easy to strain muscles and tendons. Pain is generally located about two inches below the knee along the front of the shin. Osgood-Schlatter disease generally goes away on its own in one to two years. If you have repeated or constant pain, you should see a doctor who can diagnose the cause of the pain.

Treatment

The first treatment for Osgood-Schlatter disease is to stop vigorous exercise and apply heat or ice to the sore area. Basically, you have to rest the damaged tissue until it heals. Stretching may help, and specific exercises can strengthen the bone, cartilage, and tendons of your knees and reduce your risk of a flare-up. If the attack is severe enough, you may have to wear a cast or brace on your leg. The disease occurs most commonly after participation in activities that involve fast side-to-side movement and jumping, such as basketball or volleyball, which put heavy strains on the knee and tendons.

Scoliosis

Scoliosis is a sideways deformation of the backbone in which the spine grows with a curve to the side rather than straight. Scoliosis involves abnormalities of the vertebrae, muscles, and nerves of the spine. It is most often congenital, meaning that it is present at birth, though it can develop during childhood. It usually becomes apparent between ages ten and sixteen, and needs to be evaluated by a doctor. Only a small number of people with scoliosis need treatment. Wearing a back brace is the most common treatment, though surgery is needed in some cases. If treatment is needed, it is important to obtain it as early as possible to avoid problems later in life. More girls than boys have scoliosis.

Arthritis

Arthritis is thought of as a disease that old people get, but children and adolescents can get arthritis, too. While arthritis is not directly related to growth issues, it can change how we grow and live. Arthritis is an inflammation of the joints that is often accompanied by external swelling, pain, stiffness, and redness.

The most common cause of arthritis in children and adolescents is infection. If an infection damages the growth plates, it can delay or stop growth. About one in a thousand children suffer from chronic (persistent) arthritis during the early years of their lives, with the disease commonly beginning between their first and fourth birthdays. It can, however, strike at any time. The disease is called juvenile rheumatoid arthritis (JRA) in the United States and Canada.

The most common symptom of JRA is pain, swelling, and stiffness in the joints that persists for six weeks or longer. JRA may also cause a rash and a fever, though neither tends to last long, arriving and disappearing quickly. Treatments often involve nonsteroidal anti-inflammatory drugs such as ibuprofen (found in Motrin, Advil, and Nuprin) and naproxen or naproxen sodium (found in Aleve). The goal of treatment is to maintain a high level of physical function in the joints so that the afflicted child or adolescent is able to interact socially and have a good quality of life.

Dwarfism and Genetic Short Stature

"I hear somebody on the street yell, 'Look at the midget!' and I try not to turn around. They say it like I've done something wrong, like I'm not a real person," Evan said. "They act like I'm a toy."

"They don't think we're people," Carla said. "I'm a senior, the same as Evan. We're both going to begin college next year. People I don't know look past me. They often refuse to meet my eyes. Even this year, I've had some jerk pick me up and say what a little doll I was and how cute I was."

Evan has the most common form of dwarfism, achondroplasia. He has the classic "dwarf" build, with very short arms and legs and an average sized trunk. He is less than four feet tall. In college he plans to study a combination of computers and history. Carla is a pituitary dwarf, whose limbs and body are in the same proportion as a person who is not a dwarf, but she too is less than four feet tall.

"I like both computers and history," Evan said. "I don't want to lock myself into an intellectual box during college any more than I let people do that to me because I'm short."

"Little kids are really interested in me," Carla said. "I'm almost an adult, but they're as tall as I am.

When they come up to me and ask what I am, why I'm short, I don't mind telling them. They're too open for me to cut them down. But I know some people with short stature who don't like to talk to kids about it."

"What's really interesting is the way the parents act," Evan said. "Most of them get nervous. They're afraid the kids will embarrass me or make me mad. As long as they are truly just curious, and not making fun of me, I talk to them if I have time.

"I've had trouble with some students at school," Evan continued. "But I don't have much trouble after people get to know me. I'm on the debate team and help out with a lot of projects at school. The way people act is a litmus test to identify jerks. I have too many things to do to let them get to me.

"There can be an advantage in being different from other people. It's a real minor thing, but in my family, I'm the only one who is short. My sister and brother are both of normal height. Last year, my brother told me that he used to be jealous of me. No one remembered his name or who he was. Everybody we met remembered me and knew me.

"One thing I know for sure is that I'm lucky to be living today. A hundred years ago about the only thing I could have done was go into some kind of entertainment business, like a freak show. Today, while I'll never play in the NFL, I can really do anything I want to do. I can be what I want to be."

"I'm still not sure what I want to do after college, or even in college," Carla said. "But I am going to do something that matters, that makes a difference in the

world. My attitude is that the world better get ready for me, because I'm here and I'm coming at it."

The Language of Short Stature

In the past the term "midget" was commonly used to describe a person of short stature, whose body parts had the same proportions of a person of average height. In this usage, a "midget's" arms, legs, trunk, and head would each make up about the same percentage of their total height as with other people. "Midget" is still commonly used today, but many people with short stature consider midget objectionable. Our language is changing, gladly, in an effort to help people and to not degrade them with terms that can hurt.

The term "dwarf," on the other hand, was used to describe a person with short stature whose body was not of medically normal proportions. Dwarfs, in traditional usage, had very short legs and arms, fairly average sized trunks, and heads that appeared to be too large for the rest of their bodies.

Today, physicians use "dwarf" to describe all forms of short stature, including people with profound short stature or genetically short stature. Unlike many racial terms which are inherently offensive because they have been used to degrade people, the reasons why the terms "midget" and "dwarf" are acceptable or unacceptable is harder to explain. Some people of short stature still use both words and are not bothered by either. The reality appears to be that "midget" has been used far more by people of average stature in an insulting way. The semantic (study of words) argument is that the use of midget changes the person being called a midget into an object, into something less than fully human.

Language is logical and can be analyzed objectively. However, language is often a matter involving emotions, because words strike our hearts. Words do hurt; we all know they do. The propriety of using terms like midget (or dwarf) is a matter of the emotional comfort or discomfort of the person to which they are applied. We all know the gnawing pain that comes when we are insulted and the anger that can follow.

We all know that it is simply not right to intentionally inflict that pain on other people. If the issue comes up when you meet a person of short stature, ask him or her which term he or she prefers. Ask politely, and ask with respect, but ask.

"Dwarfism" is still widely used, including on the Web site of the the Little People of America (LPA), an organization founded by people of short stature to help each other. The LPA says that the following are acceptable terms: dwarf, little person, LP, and person of short stature. The LPA adds, "Most people would rather be referred to by their name than by a label."

The Nature of Dwarfism/Short Stature

Doctors examine many adolescents with short stature, but 95 percent of those adolescents are considered late bloomers—meaning that they have started puberty later than their peers—or their parents are short. If you are a late bloomer and your parents are of average height, in almost all cases you will catch up. You might keep growing until you are in your twenties, but in the end growth does tend to average out. The differences in the rate of growth can make your life frustrating, however.

Less than 5 percent of the short kids seen at one major hospital have either hormone deficiencies that limited their growth, or genetic short stature. The genetic forms of short stature are rare. Only a few of the forms of genetic short stature can be treated in a manner that will lead to normal growth. Treatment is important, however, to help with other medical problems that often accompany dwarfism. (See the "Facing Life" section on page 60 for a discussion of the medical problems associated with dwarfism.) If there is any risk of genetic dwarfism from a deficiency in growth hormone, a physical examination should be carried out by a physician or a pediatric endocrinologist who is a growth specialist. When a deficiency in growth hormone is caught early, the condition can be treated and the individual will likely reach his or her genetic height potential.

General Causes of Dwarfism/ Short Stature

Dwarfism and short stature can be caused by a number of medical problems. The most common causes are genetic. Various parts of the endocrine system such as the pituitary and thyroid glands can fail to function properly early in childhood. Severe injury, such as multiple breaks in a leg, can also lead to short stature, and chronic illness can drain the strength we need to grow as the body puts its resources to use fighting the illness. Finally, kidney disease, difficulty absorbing nutrients because of digestive problems, and a number of other factors can lead to short stature.

Types of Dwarfism/Short Stature

The Little People of America defines dwarfism as an adult male or female whose full-growth height is four feet ten inches or shorter. This definition also requires that the short stature is caused by a medical or genetic condition.

Today there are 876 different types of dwarfism. Some types have not yet been fully identified and medically described. Our knowledge of human genetics, however, is growing at an increasingly fast pace, and the new knowledge we are gaining means that we understand more and more about the genetic causes of short stature. All of the forms of dwarfism cannot be discussed here, but the major forms are outlined below.

One term that is used often to discuss dwarfism is dysplasia. Dysplasia is the abnormal development of bone, skin, or other tissue. When applied to dwarfism, we talk about skeletal dysplasia because the bones have not developed normally. Dwarfism involving skeletal dysplasia usually results in limbs that are far shorter in proportion than in a normally developed individual. People with dysplasia are the classic dwarfs, as the term was used historically.

Achondroplasia

Achondroplasia accounts for nearly half of all cases of profound short stature. With achondroplastic dwarfism, the trunk of the body is of average size while the arms and legs are short, as are the fingers and toes. The head is slightly enlarged with a prominent forehead. Adult achondroplastic dwarfs are, on average, four feet tall. As the child grows, his or her legs assume a typical bow-legged (varus) appearance.

About 75 percent of achondroplastic dwarfs are born to normally sized parents, at a rate of between one in 26,000 and one in 40,000 births. A person with achondroplasia has a 50/50 chance of having children with the disease.

Congenital Adrenal Hyperplasia

Congenital adrenal hyperplasia prevents the adrenal glands, which are on top of the kidneys, from producing one of several hormones that the body needs to sustain life. Treatment involves replacement of the hormones the body cannot produce and must be continued throughout life. In some cases, surgery is also needed.

Congenital adrenal hyperplasia has a number of serious medical problems associated with it. About one in 10,000 people are born with this genetic condition, which is inherited from both parents. Because both parents must have the gene in order to pass it on, congential adrenal hyperplasia is a carrier disease. If only one parent carries the gene, the child will not have the disease. If both parents are carriers there is a 25 percent chance that their child will inherit defective genes from them both and have the disease. (There is also a 25 percent chance that the child will not have the disease.) The child has a 50 percent chance of inheriting one normal and one defective gene, and becoming a carrier.

Growth-Hormone Deficiency

Growth-hormone deficiency is the form of dwarfism in which the body is of normal proportion, but stature is very short. People with this disease were once called midgets. It is also known as hypopituitary dwarfism, pituitary dwarfism, or by several other terms. Between

10,000 and 15,000 people in the United States have the disease. Early identification and treatment is very important to ensure that a child with the condition grows to his or her normal height. Treatment must begin well before the growth plates in the child's bones have hardened during puberty. If the growth plates have hardened, no further growth will be possible.

The condition can be present from birth (congenital) because of abnormal formation of the pituitary or hypothalamus before birth. It may also be acquired as a result of damage to the glands during or after birth, or from a severe head injury, or may be caused by a tumor on the hypothalamus or pituitary gland. In tumor-related cases, a surgeon generally removes the tumor.

To restore normal growth, growth hormone deficiency has to be treated by giving injections of growth hormone. Injection treatment can be prescribed for three to four times per week or sometimes every day. Treatment has to continue over a number of years.

Precocious Puberty
Precocious puberty means that puberty starts earlier than normal, as does the growth spurt that comes with puberty. Children with precocious puberty may well be taller than their peers because of their early growth. However, as their bone growth is more advanced, they actually have less time to grow and may end up with short stature as adults.

Treatment of precocious puberty includes medication which can temporarily delay puberty, thus decreasing the rate of bone growth. The result is to restore the normal growth rate in the child.

Exercise

One of the major questions that arises is how much exercise is all right for someone who has a form of dwarfism. Within the limits of their medical conditions, they can indeed exercise, and healthy dwarf children can play normally.

The best exercises for people with skeletal dysplasia are those that place the least strain on their spines. Swimming and bicycling are recommended.

The Special Issues of Dwarfism

The dwarf community today faces two issues due to advances in medical care and genetics. The first involves the use of genetic testing to identify, and then abort, fetuses found to have one of the genetic markers for dwarfism. The second involves surgical lengthening of the limbs.

Genetic Testing

The first question that comes up when considering genetic testing is whether or not dwarfism is a disability. The LPA notes that there is a debate on the issue within the dwarf community. Dwarfism is covered by the Americans with Disabilities Act, and clearly many of the medical problems that accompany dwarfism—mainly bone and skeletal-related problems—can be disabling and restrict activity. However, it is those problems, not short stature itself, that cause the disability.

Genetic testing can be used to identify a condition while a fetus is in the womb. If we assume that abortion is justified in cases where genetic conditions are so severe that they result in inevitable and painful death within days or months, preventing that pain would be the right thing to do according to many people. Even if we disagree with abortion, we can understand the desire to prevent suffering.

Genes causing many forms of dwarfism have been identified, including the gene for the most common form of dwarfism, achondroplasia. The achondroplasia gene was discovered in 1994, and others were quickly discovered afterward. There was immediate debate within the dwarf community and the Little People of America whether to test fetuses of dwarf parents for the genes that would tell if it would also be a dwarf. If testing were found positive for dwarfism, should the fetus be aborted to save the baby from a life of physical pain that would end in early death?

The LPA reports on its Web site, "The common thread throughout the discussions was that we as short statured individuals are productive members of society who must inform the world that, though we face challenges, most of them are environmental (as with people with other disabilities), and we value the opportunity to contribute a unique perspective to the diversity of our society."

Environmental factors, such as the height of ATM machines, can be managed, and people who have various forms of dwarfism work at most jobs with equal productivity as anyone else. The debate over gene testing and what to do with the knowledge obtained from testing will continue for many years.

Limb Lengthening

One of the most dramatic therapies used to treat dwarfism is the surgical lengthening of arms and legs. This process requires numerous operations spread over several years.

Recovery from these surgeries is painful and requires extended physical therapy.

During limb lengthening the bones of the arms and legs are placed in a metal framework and cut. The ends of the bones are then forced apart, and new bone gradually fills in the gap, lengthening the bones. Generally, the LPA appears to be opposed to limb lengthening because it does nothing to help the underlying conditions that cause back, joint, and other orthopedic problems for dwarfs. There is also evidence that lengthened limbs are made weaker than they were originally. (As a general rule, when the body heals traumatic damage such as a broken bone or torn muscle, the new tissue is weaker than the original tissue.)

The LPA notes that the parents of dwarfs who elect to put their children through these operations do so because they do not want their children to be treated differently from any other children. This choice then is cosmetic and psychological. For that reason, many LPA members and health professionals believe that limb-lengthening operations should only be done if they have a real chance of improving health.

The LPA says that "Dwarfism is a genetic difference, not a disease, and many dwarfs are proud of not being like everyone else. Oftentimes a fourteen-year-old child who, because of teenage insecurity and peer pressure, wants his limbs lengthened will mature into an adult who is proud of who he is." On the other hand, a number of people who have had their limbs lengthened are satisfied with the results. One man mentioned by the LPA increased his height from three feet eleven inches to five feet one inch tall, which is quite dramatic. The LPA recommends that before anyone has limb-lengthening surgery, he or she should be fully evaluated by physicians regarding a number of medical issues, including a variety of alternative treatments.

Facing Life

People with various forms of dwarfism face a number of potentially serious medical problems. People with dysplasia and its underlying skeletal abnormalities often have trouble breathing, especially at night. Their throats are smaller than they need to be, and as a result can be blocked easily, and they may need to have their air passages opened. Breathing aids, such as ventilators and breathing masks that force air into their lungs, can be used to reduce the risk of serious breathing problems while sleeping.

With some forms of dwarfism, the nose and throat are narrowed, which seems to limit ventilation of the inner ear, which in turn leads to ear infections. If untreated, these infections can cause hearing damage.

Operations are often simply part of life for people with many forms of dwarfism, in large part because of the skeletal problems that are inherent with their condition. Back surgery to relieve compression of the spine is common.

If you have a form of dwarfism, the most important point is how you face life. One mother of a high school girl with dwarfism—who is herself a dwarf—sees her daughter doing what she wants at school: going to dances, joining clubs, and being fully involved in life. "I let myself be more isolated. I saw my dwarfism as limiting what I could do. I held myself back. My daughter is not doing that to herself."

The Americans with Disabilities Act and the efforts of our society are working to remove barriers facing people with handicaps and are making life easier to mange for people with short stature. Lowering ATMs to allow people in wheelchairs easier access, for example, also helps people of short stature.

Many elements of society, including colleges and employers, may instinctively wish to exclude people who are of short stature because they don't fit in with the rest of society. But overall, jobs and the future are opening up for everyone who is different from people who look "normal." Some dwarf still go into acting or other forms of entertainment, but now they do so because they choose to, not because society has blocked all other options.

Gigantism and Very Tall Stature

"My cousin and I used to shoot hoops at the park. We had been doing it since we were kids," said Josepha. "Gary was about five years older than I was, but he didn't mind playing with me." Josepha is sixteen and over six feet tall. Her arms are long and so are her hands; she can easily grip a basketball with one hand.

"Gary got a university scholarship to play basketball, but he really went to study engineering. He wanted to end up working for NASA in the space program." Josepha lowered her head and stared at the floor, speaking softly. "He died. He was just twenty-one.

"He was playing in his first basketball game of the season. He'd had to miss the first two games because of a sore knee. We had gone over to the court to watch him play. He was charging the basketball. Then he stopped, and just collapsed. The doctor got right to him, but Gary was dead. Later, they said his aorta—the big blood vessel that connects to the heart—burst. He died in seconds.

"My mother was tall. She died when I was twelve. She was only thirty-two. Both Mom and Gary had a genetic disease called Marfan's syndrome. So do I.

"I asked my doctor, 'What happens now?' Josepha's uncertainty about the future showed on her face for an instant. Then she smiled. "I have to take it easy *until we're sure about my heart. I had a picture taken of my heart last week, and my aorta is larger than it should be, but not in danger of breaking. My heart valves are in bad shape. The doctors can replace the valves and patch my aorta if they have to. I should live a pretty normal life.*

"The important thing is that I know about it. I know I have Marfan's," Josepha said. "I'll be OK. I'm going to medical school. Maybe I can do more to fight Marfan's someday." Josepha looked up. "But I really wish Mom and Gary had known they had Marfan's. They would still be here. I think of both of them. I think of Mom when I'm alone at night. That's when I miss her most. I miss Gary when I see the hoop. I can't watch basketball on TV."

Are We Taller Today Than Our Ancestors?

Modern men and women would tower over people who lived hundreds or thousands of years ago. At least, according to common belief we would. But are people living today giants compared to their ancestors?

The short answer to a tall issue is that people living in industrialized parts of the world today—North America, Europe, and Japan—are approximately four inches (ten centimeters) taller than people who lived 150 years ago. But are people taller because the human race is evolving rapidly? No. Human evolution is, at this point in the history of our species, stable. We are well adapted for how and where we live, and evolution does not account for our recent increase in height. So why are we taller? A look at recent history gives us a likely answer.

The increase in our height has not been steady. We remained about the same height from the Stone Age hundreds of thousands of years ago until the 1800s. Our recent growth has leveled off and we do not seem to be getting any taller.

While our genes are the most important factor in determining why some people are shorter or taller than other people, how well children eat is important in determining whether or not they reach their potential height.

Most scientists who study the issue believe that better childhood nutrition is the most important reason that we are taller than we were in the recent past. This also helps explain why people in developed countries are generally taller than people in underdeveloped countries. We also know that when people in developed nations suffer from famine, such as during World War I and World War II in parts of Europe, the average height among people declines. Consequently, genes serve as the blueprint for how tall we might become, while nutrition and other environmental conditions determine if we achieve our potential height.

Being tall is seldom a major problem in modern society. If anything, everybody wants to be tall. As a result, doctors seldom see patients worried about being too tall. Most people who are tall have tall parents. If you are taller than your schoolmates, it can sometimes be hard, but the thing to remember is that most likely your peers will catch up with you. Some of the medical conditions that lead to abnormally tall stature have underlying medical problems associated with them that need to be treated as soon as possible to control the disease or prevent additional damage, however.

Giants Walk the Earth, and They Always Have

We have always had stories of giants living in society. In Greek mythology, a race of giants—the Titans—lived before human beings, and one of them, Atlas, held up the world. In another example, the entrance to the royal chapel in Bangkok, Thailand, is guarded by statues of a mythological race of giants, the Yakshas. They guard the building from evil. Tales of giants fill the stories of many people around the world.

David and Goliath

The biblical story of David and Goliath dates to 3,000 years ago, when war raged in the Middle East. David was a shepherd in Israel, and Goliath was the champion from Israel's enemies, the Philistines. According to the story, Goliath was nine feet tall. He challenged the Israelite army to send a champion to fight him, with the freedom or slavery of the two nations to be decided by the outcome of the fight.

When you remember that poor nutrition made it likely that most people living in the ancient world were four or five inches shorter on average than we are, it means that Goliath could easily have been three feet taller than David. Goliath came for battle in full armor, with breastplate, helmet, and shield. David refused to wear armor, saying that it would only slow him down and make it impossible for him to fight. He was armed with a sling that let him toss stones with great force and accuracy.

When the fight began, David ran forward and used his sling to send a rock into Goliath's forehead, bringing him to the ground. David then used his sword to kill his enemy.

While the story says much about the advantages of speed in many situations, it may also be our earliest record of the medical condition of gigantism.

Modern Giants and Medical Discoveries

Being nine feet tall may be pushing the biological limits of human height, but we do have medical records of modern men suffering from gigantism who were nearly that tall. The tallest man whose height was reliably recorded was Robert Pershing Wadlow, who lived from 1918 to 1940. When he died, his body was measured at eight feet, eleven and three-quarter inches tall. The tallest woman reliably recorded was Zeng Jinlian, who lived from 1964 to 1982. When she died, she had severe scoliosis, so her full height had to be estimated. Had she been able to stand up straight, she would have been an inch or two over eight feet tall.

Historically, gigantism and acromegaly were grouped together, and acromegaly is still used by some people when speaking of both conditions. However, as we have learned more about the causes of the disorders in recent years, doctors have distinguished between them. They are now defined on the basis of whether they strike before or after the hardening of the growth plates. (See the "Gigantism and Acromegaly" section for a full discussion of the differences.) People with gigantism and acromegaly usually have tunnel vision, meaning that they can only see straight ahead and have to turn their heads to see to the sides. (Their tunnel vision is caused by the same tumor on their pituitary gland that caused their gigantism.) Without the peripheral vision that allows most of us to detect motion far to the side without turning our heads, Goliath would have been an easy target for David. David very likely ran toward the giant from the side. Once close enough, he was able to hurl his stone with deadly effect. Goliath probably never saw him coming.

Andre the Giant

The most famous "giant" of recent years was Andre Rousimoff, who wrestled professionally as Andre the Giant. (You can see Andre in the film *The Princess Bride*.) Andre was born and raised on a farm in southern France. By the age of twelve he was six feet three inches tall and weighed over two hundred pounds. Because of his gigantism, he continued to grow throughout his life, and was seven feet five inches tall and weighed over 525 pounds when he died at age forty-six in 1993. Andre died prematurely because his body grew too large to support itself, and his heart finally failed.

Modern treatments of gigantism did not exist when Andre was born in 1947 or when he was growing up in the 1950s. Andre was an intelligent man living in a body that led many people to assume he was not bright. The hulking appearance that resulted from his disease matched too many prejudices. Also, growing up on a farm in a rural part of France—especially in the years immediately after World War II—he had few options. He became a professional wrestler, first in Europe and then in America.

Had he been born today, Andre would probably have been treated for his condition. He would have still been a tall man, but not a giant, and his body would not have worn out in middle age.

Gigantism and Acromegaly

Gigantism is very rare. About six people out of every 100,000 will have acromegaly. Most gigantism and acromegaly are caused by the chronic presence of too much growth hormone in the body, and both are often caused by a benign (noncancerous) tumor on the pituitary gland. The tumor causes the pituitary gland to produce too much growth hormone. A small number of cases may be caused by tumors in other organs. (In some cases, not enough growth hormone will be produced because of a tumor, leading to short stature rather than great height.) The excess growth hormone stimulates the liver to produce another hormone, insulin-like growth factor 1 (IGF-1) that is in turn directly responsible for the rapid growth.

People often use the term "acromegaly" to refer to people with both gigantism and acromegaly, but we should be more accurate. Whether too much growth hormone leads to gigantism and acromegaly depends upon when the problem happens. If it occurs before the growth plates have hardened and stopped producing new bone—before the end of puberty—the individual will suffer from gigantism. With gigantism, the bones—especially the long bones of the arms and legs—continue to grow throughout the person's life. They keep getting taller and taller.

If the excess growth hormone occurs after the growth plates have hardened, the condition is called acromegaly. Acromegaly does involve some growth of bone and connective tissue, but with the bones increasing in diameter rather then length. The condition becomes most apparent in the increased size and heaviness of the fingers, toes, hands, and feet, and in the heaviness of the jaw and face.

Because the extra growth hormone that causes acromegaly starts after the growth plates have ossified (turned to bone), the person does not grow taller.

Treatment

Both gigantism and acromegaly can be treated today by one of two methods. The first method is through surgery to remove the tumor on the pituitary that causes the condition. The second method of treatment is to use radiation to treat the tumor. In some cases, the tumor is so large that it cannot be entirely removed. Doctors must then try to remove enough of the tumor to prevent further damage to the patient's vision and then use drugs to limit the impact of the excess growth hormone that might still be produced. Treatments usually bring the condition under control, returning normal growth.

Marfan's Syndrome

In 1896, French physician Antoni Marfan first documented the clinical signs of the syndrome that was later named after him. Marfan's syndrome is caused by a single defect on a single one of our chromosomes (Chromosome 15). Marfan's affects the connective tissue fibrillin, making it weaker than it should be. Connective tissue provides support for organs of the body and helps "glue" us together. It also determines how flexible the organs, bones, and ligaments are.

Fibrillin is used in many places in the human body, including the skeleton, lungs, eyes, heart, and blood vessels. Because of Marfan's, the connective tissue of the heart, lungs, eyes, and skeletal system can stretch and weaken. Marfan's affects most seriously the cardiovascular system, the heart, and blood vessels.

People with Marfan's syndrome do not become giants as do those with gigantism, but they are often very tall and very thin. Typically, they have long, thin arms, legs, hands, and feet. Their chests can have either a prominent sternum (breastbone) or a slight indentation over the breastbone. They also tend to have a narrow, arched palate (roof of the mouth).

Marfan's is passed from parent to child, and children of people with Marfan's have a 50/50 chance of inheriting the syndrome. Estimates vary, but between 5 and 30 percent of Marfan's cases happen because of a random mutation (change) in the gene, and not because a parent had the disorder.

Approximately 200,000 people in the United States have Marfan's syndrome or a related disorder. The most common estimate for the frequency of Marfan's is that one out of every 10,000 people has the condition. Some estimates, however, say as many as one in 5,000 or one in 3,000 people might have Marfan's. The problem is that many people with the syndrome simply do not realize that they have Marfan's and have never been diagnosed with it.

Harmful Effects of Marfan's

Marfan's patients often have a defect in their aorta, which is the main artery in the body. It carries blood directly from the left side of the heart, and then branches to form the other arteries in the body. In Marfan's, the aorta is weak and can balloon to several times its normal diameter before bursting. The ballooning is called an aneurysm; in this case, an aortic aneurysm.

The second common heart defect found in Marfan's patients is a weakness in one of the heart valves. The mitral valve is between the left atrium and left ventricle chambers of the heart. The left and right atriums are the upper chambers of the heart, while the ventricles are the heart's two lower chambers. Two flaps of tissue form the mitral valve. The valve should only open in the direction of the proper flow of blood, preventing blood from flowing backward and lessening the efficiency of the heart's pumping action. With Marfan's, the flaps forming the valve may billow backwards, leading to irregular heartbeats or to heart failure that can cause death.

Because of the defect in their aortas and valves, most Marfan's patients in the past have died quite young, sometimes even in their late teens or early twenties. Modern medical procedures are now available to repair both defects with surgery.

Modern Signs of Marfan's

Marfan's was not well known at all until the sudden death of several famous athletes in the early 1980s. Flo Hyman was a member of the U.S. Olympic women's volleyball team that won a silver medal in the 1984 games. She collapsed and died in 1986 during a game. At about the same time, two University of Maryland basketball players also died while playing the game they loved. All died because of heart defects caused by Marfan's syndrome.

Marfan's Treatment

While there is no cure for Marfan's, the damage caused by the syndrome can be treated. Treatment is especially important for life-threatening defects in the heart and aorta. Drugs are used first to reduce the stress placed on the heart. A class of drugs called beta-blockers has proven effective in reducing this stress.

Both the valve defects and the weakness of the aorta are essentially mechanical problems. When the conditions worsen, they can be repaired with surgery. The repair of the aorta involves grafting (sewing) a patch onto the aorta. The valves are patched or replaced in a similar way. Doctors now recommend using an echocardiogram to take sound pictures of the heart. Repairs can be made before a dangerous defective valve places too much strain on the heart, further weakening it, or before the aorta bursts.

People with Marfan's often have poor eyesight and are usually myopic (nearsighted). The lenses of their eyes may also be off center, as it is the connective tissue in the eye that holds the lens in place. It is important for Marfan's patients to have an eye examination at least once a year. With Marfan's, there is an increased risk of a number of eye problems, including glaucoma, cataracts, and retina detachment.

Living With Marfan's

Janis Cortese has Marfan's syndrome and maintains a Web site that talks about the syndrome and how she has coped with the disease. She points out that she has to limit her exercise and argues that Marfan's patients should avoid contact sports entirely. Janis says that the body joints of all Marfan's patients can be easily damaged because of the weakness in the connective tissue that underlies Marfan's. Medical professionals generally agree with this assessment.

Equally susceptible to damage are the lenses of the eyes, which are held in place less firmly than they should be, and could be dislodged by a blow to the head. Above all, activity that increases blood pressure could further damage the heart or lead to a rupture in the aorta.

Scuba diving and flying in an unpressurized plane are things Janis cannot do because the tissues that hold her lungs to her chest wall are weak and the lungs themselves are not as strong as they should be. People with Marfan's also need to watch their diets carefully and have to take good care of their teeth to lessen the risk of dental troubles.

Because people with Marfan's can both be taller than average and have longer arms and legs, finding clothes that fit properly can be difficult and frustrating. Pants purchased at a regular store, for example, can look as if they are capri pants. Janis recommends a number of online stores on her Web site. If you live in a large town or city, there is a good chance you can find stores that specialize in clothes for tall people.

Facing the Expectations of Others and of Ourselves

Elizabeth

"You have to play with their minds sometimes," Elizabeth said. "I'm small, petite—to make it sound polite. Even now that I'm sixteen and finished with puberty, I'm only a few inches over five feet tall. People would come up to me and think I was a lot younger than I was. I was cute and blonde and tiny." Elizabeth laughed. "I had to let them know I'm not all that cute.

"Sometimes people still patronize me. Usually, it's an adult who is being self-important," she said. "They'll be talking to me like I was still a kid. Delicate. Not very bright. I'll look at them and smile, and tell them to stop acting like an idiot. Most of them kind of jerk back in shock. Every now and then they see what's happening and look just a bit ashamed of themselves."

Aaron

Aaron's parents are both tall, and he is matching them in growth. He did not start puberty any earlier than most of his friends, but he was always taller than they were. Aaron is in high school now, and he is still taller than most of his friends.

"When I was in middle school, I was almost six feet tall," Aaron said. "I'd be playing with my friends, running around and climbing over stuff and having fun, and some adult would start glaring at me. Sure, I seemed to knock things over a lot more than other kids, but I didn't mean to. I'm not a jock and have never been very coordinated. I always felt really off balance growing up.

"It took me a long time to figure out why most of the adults I was around expected me to act like an adult. Unless they knew me, they thought I was in high school, maybe even college. They looked at me and saw what they expected to see, a person a lot older than I was. I can't be responsible for what they thought, or what they expected me to do. I was doing the best I could, and I still am."

Paige

"I started puberty late," Paige said. "I was the shortest kid in my class in eighth grade. I had no boobs at all, and didn't really understand when the other girls had boyfriends they talked about all the time. Boys still seemed to be lame. I couldn't talk to my old friends about anything important anymore.

"Maybe my puberty was late because I've always been athletic. Maybe it was just me." Paige is now a junior—tall, with long brown hair. "I hated having to step back from the other kids so I didn't have to bend my neck to look up at them.

"All through middle school, I kept asking why I wasn't growing, why I didn't have breasts yet. I should have been as tall as my friends. I kept looking in the mirror trying to see some sign I was starting *puberty and would grow. I even kind of hoped I'd see a zit.*

"Over the next summer, I grew five inches! When I walked into ninth grade, I could look people in the eyes. Kids who had been way taller then me used to stare down at me. Now, they even took a step back, like they were giving me more respect.

"I grew two more inches that year. I loved every inch that I grew. I couldn't believe it. Sometimes, I still don't. When I first get up in the morning and look in the mirror as I get dressed, I don't recognize myself. Inside, I still see me as short."

To be alive is to be uncertain. We want to know what happens next, but we never can. Because of the unknown, it is always surprising when some adults cannot, or will not, remember what it was like to be a teenager. Perhaps they are taking refuge in their own images of being an adult. Maybe life has worn them down and they seek shelter in a comfortable rut. The best of us seek new things, new ideas, and new experiences. It is the "new" in life that keeps our minds growing and our bodies alive.

At the same time, we all share some basic fears and anxieties. We are happy to belong because we want to be part of some group, but we are also quick to exclude some people because they are different from ourselves. We need to be alone at times, yet fear being alone all of the time, or being abandoned by our friends and family. Part of what happens to us all is that we do not really see ourselves. We see the image of ourselves, our memories of what we look like.

The experience Paige talked about, of thinking of herself as being short even though she has grown to be nearly six feet tall, shows the same thing. Our images of ourselves reflect our past but seldom our present. In addition, we believe that some things determine what other people think of us. But how tall we are, how fat or how thin, how we look, usually makes no real difference to our friends. The physical differences between us mainly let us identify each other as individuals. Paige said something else later in her conversation:

"I used to be very shy. I wouldn't talk to people and kept to myself, and no one talked to me. People say someone is 'painfully shy,' and that was me. It hurt too much to open up. There was no way I could talk to people outside of my family and a few close friends.

"Then, a couple of years ago, something happened. I don't know why. It was right before I started to grow. I realized all of a sudden that people not talking to me had nothing do to with whether they liked me or not. They didn't know me enough to like me or not like me.

"The problem was that I was projecting my own shyness and uncertainty out to the world and to people, and that kept people away from me. I said to myself that if I didn't change, I would be lonely— and alone—all of my life. I wasn't going to let that happen. I couldn't.

"The shy person is still there, nagging at me from somewhere in my mind, but that's where she's going to stay. You can't let how you look control who you are."

Glossary

acromegaly A medical condition caused by too much growth hormone in the body, after the growth plates have hardened. The result is larger bones in hands, feet, jaw, and face, but without an increase in height.

adolescence The years between the end of childhood and adulthood; the early teenage years.

artery One of the blood vessels that carries blood from the heart to the body.

congenital andrenal hyperplasia A condition preventing the adrenal glands from producing a certain type of hormone, resulting in dwarfism.

dysplasia The abnormal development of bone, skin, or other tissue.

echocardiogram A medical device that uses sound waves to create a picture of the body.

epiphyseal plates or **epiphysis** The growth plates at the ends of our bones.

estrogen A major female sex hormone that regulates a woman's reproductive system.

fibrillin A form of connective tissue that is affected by Marfan's syndrome.

gigantism A medical condition caused by too much growth hormone in the body. Caused by noncancerous tumors on the pituitary gland.

genetic marker A gene that has been identified as being connected to a specific disease or condition.

growth hormone A hormone produced by the pituitary gland that stimulates production of a related hormone in our livers, which in turn stimulates growth.

growth plates The epiphyseal plates or epiphysis, which are regions at the ends of our bones that convert carti-lage into bone, and usually harden by the end of puberty, stopping growth.

hormones Chemical messengers that are produced by glands and used by the body to regulate many functions.

Marfan's syndrome A condition that weakens the con-nective tissue (fibrillin) in the body. Marfan's affects the skeleton, lungs, eyes, heart, and blood vessels. Treatment is vital to prevent early death because of failure of the heart or the aorta, the major artery that carries blood from the heart.

menarche The onset of menstruation.

Osgood-Schlatter disease A common ailment in teens that causes pain and swelling in the knee or upper part of the shin. This disease usually goes away on its own in under two years.

ovaries Female sex glands that produce sex hormones.

pituitary gland A pea-sized gland located in a cavity at the base of the skull. It is the master endocrine gland, directing the action of many other glands.

puberty The physical changes that occur as adolescents become sexually mature and able to reproduce.

syndrome A collection of symptoms and medical signs that combine to create a clinical picture for doctors that identifies a specific medical disorder or condition.

testes Male sex glands that produce sex hormones.

testosterone A vital sex hormone. It is produced by the testes and also by a woman's ovaries.

tumor An abnormal mass of tissue in the body caused by the rapid and disorganized growth of cells.

Where to Go for Help

In the United States

The American Academy of Pediatrics
141 Northwest Point Boulevard
Elk Grove Village, IL 60007-1098
(847) 434-4000
Web site: http: //www.aap.org

American Anorexia Bulimia Association, Inc.
165 West 46th Street, Suite 1108
New York, NY 10036
(212) 575-6200
Web site: http://www.aabainc.org

Dwarf Athletic Association of America
418 Willow Way
Lewisville, TX 75077
(972) 317-8299
e-mail: daaa@flash.net
Web site: http://www.daaa.org

Human Growth Foundation
997 Glen Cove Ave.
Glen Head, NY 11545
(800) 451-6434
e-mail: hgf1@hgfound.org
Web site: http://www.hgfound.org

Little People of America
P.O. Box 745
Lubbock, TX 79408
(888) 572-LPA-2001 (English and Spanish)
e-mail: lpadatabase@juno.com
Web site: http://www.lpaonline.org

National Association of Anorexia Nervosa
    and Associated Disorders
P.O. Box 7
Highland Park IL 60035
(847) 831-3438
e-mail: info@anad.org
Web site: http://www.anad.org

The National Marfan Foundation
382 Main Street
Port Washington, NY 11050
(800) 8-MARFAN (862-7326)
(516) 883-8712
Web site: http://www.marfan.org

Pituitary Disorders Education and Support
Teresa Sullivan
809 Oakridge Court
Brighton, MI 48116
(810) 227-5615

e-mail: pituitary@mediaone.net
Web site: http://www.pituitarysupport.com

In Canada

Arthritis Canada
393 University Avenue, Suite 1700
Toronto, ON M5G 1E6
(416) 979-7228, extension 321
e-mail: info@arthritis.ca
Web site: http://www.arthritis.ca

Canadian Marfan Association
Centre Plaza Postal Outlet
128 Queen Street South
P.O. Box 42257
Mississauga, ON L5M 4Z0
(905) 826-3223
e-mail: info@marfan.ca
Web site: http://www.marfan.ca

Canadian Pediatric Society
100-2204 Walkley Road
Ottawa, ON K1G 4G8
(613) 526-9397
Web site: http://www.cps.ca/english/index.htm

Little People of Manitoba
c/o Vic Moore, President
680 Rosedale Avenue
Winnipeg, MB R3L 1M8
e-mail: ummagal2@cc.umanitoba.ca

Little People of Ontario
Box 43072
4841 Yonge Street
Toronto, ON M2N 6N1
e-mail: lpo@bfree.on.ca
Web site: http://www.lpo.on.ca

The National Eating Disorder Information Centre (NEDIC)
CW 1-211, 200 Elizabeth Street
Toronto, ON M5G 2C4
(416) 340-4156
e-mail: nedic@uhn.on.ca
Web site: http://www.nedic.ca

The Quebec Association for Persons of Short Stature
2177 rue Masson, Suite 205
Montréal, Québec
Canada   H2H 1B1
(514) 521-9671
e-mail: aqppt@total.net
Web site: http://www.aqppt.org

Web Sites

Janis' Marfan Syndrome Page
http://www.io.com/~cortese/marfan
Janis Cortese, who has Marfan's syndrome, maintains
 an excellent site discussing the nature of Marfan's
 and reporting how she has learned to live with
 the syndrome.

Dwarfism.org
http://www.dwarfism.org
The site is a centralized source for information and
help regarding dwarfism. There is a list of nearly
900 forms of dwarfism, a detailed list of support
organizations, and much other good information. It
also has a shopping page.

Pediatric Rheumatology Page
http://www.goldscout.com/index.html
This Web site is dedicated to helping kids with juvenile
rheumatoid arthritis and their families and physicians.
It is provided by Thomas J. A. Lehman M.D., chief of
the division of pediatric rheumatology at the hospital
for Special Surgery in New York.

For Further Reading

Alcamo, I. Edward. *The Princeton Review Anatomy Coloring Workbook*. New York: Random House, 1997.

Bell, Alison, and Lisa Rooney. *Your Body, Yourself: A Guide to Your Changing Body*. Los Angeles, CA: Lowell House Juvenile, 1996.

Benson, Michael D. *Coping with Birth Control*. New York: Hazelden/Rosen Publishing Group, 1998.

Dabbs, James McBride, and Mary Godwin Dabbs. *Heroes, Rogues, and Lovers: Testosterone and Behavior*. New York: McGraw-Hill, 2000

Franck, Irene, and David Brownstone. *Parenting A to Z: A Guide to Everything from Conception to College*. 2nd ed. New York: HarperCollins, 1996.

Gravelle, Karen, and Jennifer Gravelle. *The Period Book: Everything You Don't Want to Ask (But Need to Know)*. New York: Walker and Company, 1996.

Madaras, Linda, and Area Madaras. *My Body, My Self for Boys: For Preteens and Teens*. New York: Newmarket Press, 2000.

Madaras, Linda, and Area Madaras. *My Body, My Self for Girls: The What's Happening to My Body Workbook*. 2nd ed. New York: Newmarket Press, 2000.

McKoy, Kathy, and Charles Wibbelsman. *The New Teenage Body Book.* New York: The Body Press/Perigee, 1992.

Rinzer, Carol Ann. *Why Eve Doesn't Have an Adam's Apple: A Dictionary of Sex Differences.* New York: Facts on File, 1996.

Smith, Anthony. *Ultimate Universe: The Human Body.* New York: Discovery Books/Random House, 1998.

INDEX

About the Author

Jim W. Fiscus is a freelance writer and photojournalist based in Oregon. He has been a medical and science writer for over a decade, producing work for both physicians and the general public. Before turning to science writing full-time, he obtained a master's degree in Middle Eastern and Asian history and taught military history. He also writes about business and legal issues that affect professional writers.

Acknowledgments

I wish to thank the people who talked with me about growth and the problems they experienced or observed that were related to growth, in particular: Zoe, Sean, and Lillie Wells, Aaron Bodor, Cara Egan, Ann Hoffert, Maria Rose, Paige, Morgan, Ricky, Zack, and all the other people who let me bug them.